Enslow Publishing

INVESTIGATE!

WHO'S THE GREATEST? Sports Stars

CAITLIN CLARK VS DIANA TAURASI

KRISTEN RAJCZAK NELSON

WOMEN'S BASKETBALL'S GREATEST

Please visit our website, www.enslow.com. For a free color catalog of all our high-quality books, call toll free 1-800-398-2504 or fax 1-877-980-4454.

Cataloging-in-Publication Data

Names: Rajczak Nelson, Kristen.
Title: Caitlin Clark vs. Diana Taurasi: women's basketball's greatest / Kristen Rajczak Nelson.
Description: Buffalo, NY : Enslow Publishing, 2026. | Series: Who's the greatest?: sports stars | Includes glossary and index.
Identifiers: ISBN 9781978546868 (pbk.) | ISBN 9781978546875 (library bound) | ISBN 9781978546882 (ebook)
Subjects: LCSH: Clark, Caitlin, 2002—Biography–Juvenile literature. | Taurasi, Diana–Biography–Juvenile literature. | Women basketball players–United States–Statistics–Juvenile literature.
Classification: LCC GV884.C554 R344 2026 | DDC 796.323092–dc23

Published in 2026 by
Enslow Publishing
2544 Clinton Street
Buffalo, NY 14224

Designer: Tanya Dellaccio Keeney
Editors: Kristen Rajczak Nelson and Therese Shea

Photo credits: Cover (Clark), pp. 7, 11, 13, 27 ZUMA Press, Inc./Alamy.com; cover (Taurasi) SPP Sport Press Photo/Alamy.com; p. 5 (Clark) https://upload.wikimedia.org/wikipedia/commons/e/ec/Caitlin_Clark_Fever_%28cropped%29.jpg; p. 5 (Taurasi) https://upload.wikimedia.org/wikipedia/commons/e/e9/Diana_Taurasi_2024_%28cropped%29.jpg; p. 9 https://upload.wikimedia.org/wikipedia/commons/f/fb/Caitlin_Clark_%282%29_%28cropped%29.jpg; p. 10 Ken Wolter/Shutterstock.com; p. 14 University of College/Shutterstock.com; p. 15 https://upload.wikimedia.org/wikipedia/commons/3/36/Caitlin_Clark_Big_Ten_tournament_2024.jpg; p. 17 Cal Sports Media/Alamy.com; pp. 18, 19, 26 UPI/Alamy.com; p. 21 CTK/Alamy.com; pp. 23 (left), 29 (top) Sipa USA/Alamy.com; p. 23 (right) Hadrian/Shutterstock.com; p. 25 Sport In Pictures/Alamy.com; p. 29 (bottom) https://upload.wikimedia.org/wikipedia/commons/1/10/Caitlin_Clark_speaking_2024_%28cropped%29.jpg.

Printed in the United States of America

CPSIA compliance information: Batch #CW26ENS: For further information contact Enslow Publishing, at 1-800-398-2504.

CONTENTS

Words in the glossary appear in **bold** type the first time they are used in the text.

GOATS

Women's basketball has seen a lot of great players. But only one has scored more than 10,000 points over the course of her WNBA career: Diana Taurasi. This accomplishment proves she is one of the best ever!

But no woman has set the basketball world on fire quite like Caitlin Clark. In 2024, she became the all-time leading scorer in NCAA basketball history—male or female. At the start of her WNBA **career**, some say she's on track to be the greatest of all time!

Did You Know?

WNBA stands for Women's National Basketball Association.

IS IT POSSIBLE TO COMPARE TAURASI AND CLARK? ONE HAS JUST FINISHED HER CAREER AND THE OTHER IS JUST GETTING STARTED!

DIANA TAURASI

CAITLIN CLARK

MEET TAURASI

Diana Taurasi was born on June 11, 1982. She grew up in California with her parents, Mario and Liliana, and her older sister Jessika. They spoke both English and Spanish at home.

Taurasi played soccer and basketball while growing up. When she reached high school, she chose to make basketball her **focus**. She made her mark on the court and led her team to **compete** for the state championship, though they didn't win. As a senior, Taurasi averaged 28.8 points a game!

Did You Know?

The Naismith Prep Player of the Year Award is given to the top men's and women's high school basketball players each year.

TAURASI IS ONE OF THE HIGHEST SCORERS IN THE HISTORY OF CALIFORNIA GIRLS' HIGH SCHOOL BASKETBALL.

3,047 POINTS AS A HIGH SCHOOL BASKETBALL PLAYER

2000 NAISMITH AWARD WINNER

SET HER SCHOOL'S SINGLE SEASON 3-POINT RECORD 96 IN 1999*

*RECORD BROKEN IN 2016

MEET CLARK

Caitlin Clark was born on January 22, 2002. She lived in West Des Moines, Iowa, with her parents Anne and Brent. Clark has two brothers, Blake and Colin. Caitlin liked playing softball, soccer, golf, and tennis when she was growing up.

As she got older, her basketball talent really started to show. At Dowling Catholic High School, Clark helped her team get to the state tournament three times. As a junior, she scored 60 points in one game!

Did You Know?

Clark played soccer in high school. She led the team in scoring.

2-TIME GOLD MEDALIST WITH USA BASKETBALL UNDER-19 TEAM

2,547 POINTS AS A HIGH SCHOOL BASKETBALL PLAYER

MISS IOWA BASKETBALL 2020

MISS IOWA BASKETBALL IS AN HONOR GIVEN TO THE BEST HIGH SCHOOL GIRLS' BASKETBALL PLAYER EACH YEAR.

UCONN GREAT

Taurasi began playing for the University of Connecticut (UConn) Huskies in 2000. She joined another **future** WNBA great on the court: Sue Bird. The team went 32–3 that season. They made it to the **Final Four** but lost to Notre Dame.

Taurasi's second season with the Huskies was a great success. The team won all 39 games in the 2001–2002 season. She and Bird led the team to the NCAA Division 1 women's national championship game against the University of Oklahoma. They won 82-70.

Did You Know?

The NCAA, or National Collegiate Athletic Association, is the group that controls college sports. UConn is a Division 1 school. This is the top division, or grouping, of sports teams in the NCAA.

TAURASI WORE NUMBER 3 WITH THE HUSKIES. SHE WENT ON TO WEAR THAT NUMBER IN THE WNBA TOO.

Taurasi's third season with the Huskies was a showstopper. She averaged 17.9 points per game and led the team to a 37–1 record. But it was her play in the national championship game that put her in the spotlight. She scored 28 points, including four 3-pointers, on the way to another championship for the Huskies.

Taurasi was a force on the court in the 2003–2004 season. She led the Huskies to the NCAA women's championship yet again in 2004!

2,156 CAREER POINTS

3-TIME NCAA DIVISION 1 WOMEN'S CHAMPION (2002, 2003, 2004)

2-TIME NATIONAL PLAYER OF THE YEAR (2003, 2004)

BIG EAST PLAYER OF THE YEAR (2003, 2004)

TAURASI WAS NAMED THE FINAL FOUR MOST OUTSTANDING PLAYER IN BOTH 2003 AND 2004.

IOWA STANDOUT

A lot of colleges wanted Clark to come play for them. She chose the University of Iowa. She started playing for the Hawkeyes in 2020. She was the top scorer in Division 1 women's basketball! Clark was named the Big Ten Freshman of the Year.

The next season, Clark averaged 27 points a game, plus an average of 8 assists and 8 rebounds. Her signature long-range 3-point shots were on full display throughout the 2021–2022 season.

CLARK HAS BEEN KNOWN TO SHOOT FROM 28 FEET (8.5 M) OR MORE.

Did You Know?

The Big Ten is one **conference** in NCAA Division 1 sports. The Big East is the conference UConn is part of.

In 2023, Clark led the Hawkeyes to the NCAA women's championship game. She scored 30 points as the team faced the University of Louisville, though they lost. Almost 10 million people watched the game, in part because of Clark's incredible play throughout the season.

The following season, Clark broke the NCAA women's scoring record. Her play helped bring the Hawkeyes back to the NCAA championship game. Almost 19 million people watched Clark and the Hawkeyes lose to the University of South Carolina.

Did You Know?

Clark's jersey number, 22, was retired at the University of Iowa in 2025.

2-TIME AAU SULLIVAN AWARD WINNER (2022, 2023)

ALL-TIME NCAA BASKETBALL LEADING SCORER

CLARK NEVER WON AN NCAA CHAMPIONSHIP, BUT SHE DID SET THE RECORD FOR MOST POINTS SCORED BY ANY NCAA BASKETBALL PLAYER—MALE OR FEMALE—WHILE AT IOWA.

NCAA SINGLE-SEASON RECORD FOR 3-POINTERS

2-TIME AP WOMEN'S BASKETBALL PLAYER OF THE YEAR (2023, 2024)

DRAFT PICKS

As a kid, Taurasi dreamed of playing in the WNBA. In 2004, this dream came true. Taurasi was chosen first in the WNBA Draft by the Phoenix Mercury. Taurasi would play guard for the team based in Phoenix, Arizona.

About 2.4 million people watched the WNBA Draft in 2024—more than four times more than 2023. This was in large part due to the excitement about Clark. She was chosen first in the draft by the Indiana Fever.

NO. 1 WNBA DRAFT PICK 2004

TAURASI IS 6 FEET (1.8 M) TALL.

CLARK IS 6 FEET (1.8 M) TALL AND PLAYS GUARD.

NO. 1 WNBA DRAFT PICK 2024

Did You Know?

Right before the 2024 WNBA Draft, Clark appeared on *Saturday Night Live*!

ROOKIES

Taurasi joined the Mercury after a particularly bad season. The Mercury had just ended a season with 8 wins and 26 losses. With Taurasi, the team was able to better their record to 17–17. She averaged 17 points a game, leading the team in scoring.

Though the team didn't make the playoffs, Taurasi was still chosen for the All-WNBA First Team. She finished the season with 578 points, making her the top scorer among the WNBA rookies that year.

Did You Know?

Taurasi played in Europe between WNBA seasons for many years. In fact, she's a six-time Euroleague champion.

TAURASI HAD THE SECOND-MOST REBOUNDS AND ASSISTS AMONG WNBA ROOKIES.

WNBA ROOKIE OF THE YEAR 2004

Clark's rookie season with the Fever started out rough. She wasn't making enough shots, and the team lost more games than they won. Following a break for the Olympic Games, Clark and the Fever began winning. They turned it around enough for the Fever to make it to the playoffs for the first time since 2016.

Despite a rocky start, Clark broke records as a rookie. She recorded the most assists in a game in WNBA history!

Did You Know?

Time magazine named Clark 2024's athlete of the year. It was only the second time a woman had been given this honor on her own.

CLARK WAS THE FIRST WNBA ROOKIE TO EVER GET A TRIPLE-DOUBLE!

WNBA ROOKIE OF THE YEAR 2024

OLYMPIC DREAMS

There are two **categories** in which Taurasi and Clark can't be compared—yet. First, Taurasi holds the Olympic record for most gold medals won by a basketball player. She won gold with Team USA in 2004, 2008, 2012, 2016, 2021, and 2024. Additionally, Taurasi has led the Mercury to WNBA championships in 2007, 2009, and 2014.

Clark has made it clear that she aims to win a WNBA championship. As one of the top women's basketball players today, it's likely she'll be part of future Olympic teams too.

CLARK WAS CONSIDERED FOR THE 2024 WOMEN'S TEAM AT THE OLYMPICS BUT NOT CHOSEN. WHAT WOULD IT HAVE BEEN LIKE IF TAURASI AND CLARK SHARED THE COURT?

6-TIME OLYMPIC GOLD MEDALIST

3-TIME WNBA CHAMPION

RECORD-SETTING PLAYERS

TAURASI WNBA RECORDS

- WNBA MVP (2009)
- 10-time All-WNBA First Team
- 2-time WNBA Finals MVP
- WNBA record for scoring average in a season (25.3)
- WNBA record for points in a season (860 in 2006)
- Most 30-point games in WNBA history
- WNBA record for 3-point shots in a career (1,447)

"YOU CAN'T TELL THE STORY OF THE WNBA WITHOUT DIANA. SHE HELPED BUILD THE LEAGUE INTO WHAT IT IS TODAY."
- ADAM SILVER, NBA COMMISSIONER

CLARK WNBA RECORDS*

- WNBA record for 3-pointers made by a rookie (122)
- WNBA record for points made by a rookie (769)
- All-WNBA First Team (2024)
- Fever record for most double-doubles in a season (14)
- Fever record for most 3-pointers in a season (103)
- WNBA record for fastest player to reach 100 3-pointers
- WNBA record for assists in a single game (19)

*AS OF 2025

"WHAT CAITLIN'S BEEN ABLE TO DO IN HER SHORT CAREER SO FAR HAS BEEN NOTHING SHORT OF REMARKABLE ... SHE KEEPS GETTING BETTER EVERY SINGLE GAME. SO HER FUTURE IS SUPER BRIGHT."
- DIANA TAURASI

GIVING BACK

Both Taurasi and Clark show greatness off the court too. Taurasi has worked with a group that builds playgrounds and safe play spaces for kids across the United States. She has also given time and money to groups that **support** moms in need.

Clark founded the Caitlin Clark Foundation in 2023. Its goal is to help kids through three things Clark found important in her life: **nutrition**, education, and playing sports. Clark has also given books to schools in need and supported the Women's Sports **Foundation**.

Did You Know?

Taurasi has two kids with her wife, Penny Taylor, a former WNBA player. Becoming a mom made her want to support other mothers.

PENNY TAYLOR

IN 2025, THE CAITLIN CLARK FOUNDATION ANNOUNCED IT WAS PART OF BUILDING NEW SOCCER AND BASKETBALL COURTS AT FOUR DES MOINES PUBLIC SCHOOLS.

GLOSSARY

career: The job someone chooses to do for a long time.

category: Class or group.

compete: To try to win a contest with others.

conference: A group of sports teams that compete with each other.

Final Four: The second-to-last set of games in a playoff tournament.

focus: To direct your attention or effort to something specific.

foundation: A not-for-profit organization provided with funds to support charitable works.

future: What is to come.

nutrition: The act of being nourished.

retire: To leave a job and stop working.

support: To hold up and help.

triple-double: Getting 10 or more of three of the following in a single game: points, assists, blocks, steals, or rebounds.

FOR MORE INFORMATION

BOOKS

Nelson, Kristen Rajczak. *Diana Taurasi: Basketball GOAT.* Buffalo, NY: Gareth Stevens Publishing, 2025.

Roggio, Sarah. *Caitlin Clark vs. Cheryl Miller: Who Would Win?* Minneapolis, MN: Lerner Publications, 2026.

WEBSITES

Caitlin Clark Foundation
caitlinclarkfoundation.org
Find out more about the Caitlin Clark Foundation here.

Diana Taurasi
dianataurasi.com
Find out what Diana Taurasi is up to next on her website.

Publisher's note to educators and parents: Our editors have carefully reviewed these websites to ensure that they are suitable for students. Many websites change frequently, however, and we cannot guarantee that a site's future contents will continue to meet our high standards of quality and educational value. Be advised that students should be closely supervised whenever they access the internet.

INDEX